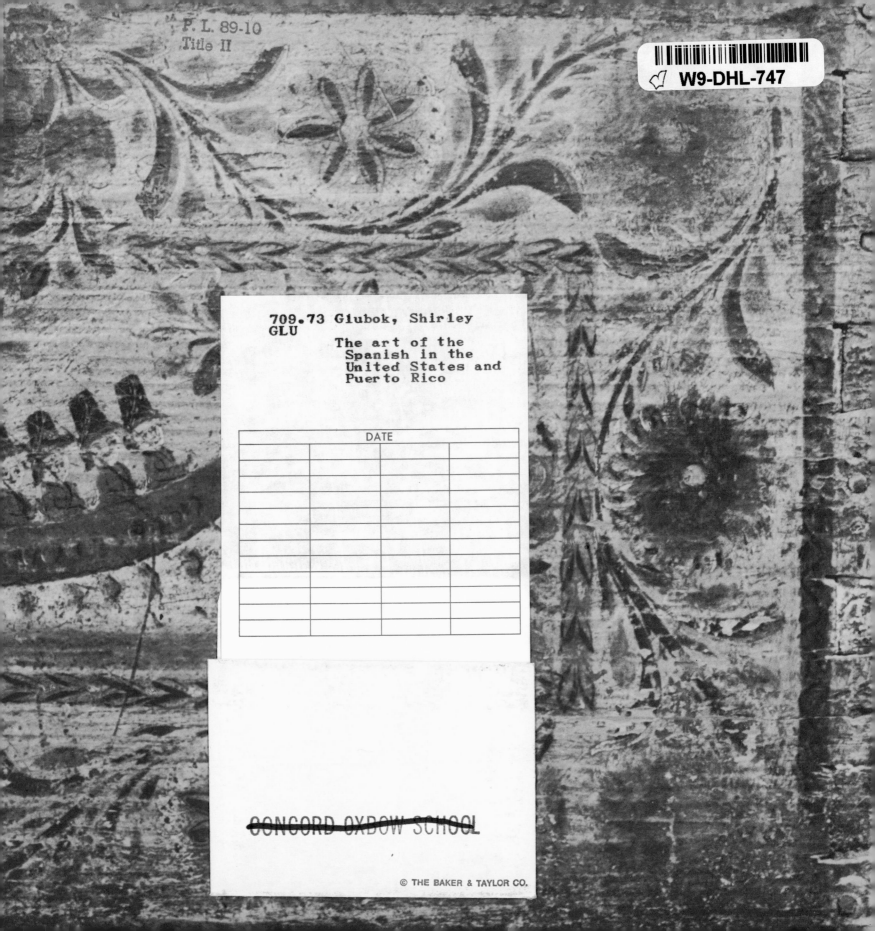

709.73 Glubok, Shirley
GLU

The art of the
Spanish in the
United States and
Puerto Rico

DATE			

the art of the SPANISH
in the united states and puerto rico

by shirley glubok

Designed by Gerard Nook
Photographs by Alfred Tamarin

The Macmillan Company, New York, New York
Collier-Macmillan Ltd., London

Santiago, Puerto Rican santo, about 1900, Collection of Teodoro Vidal

The author gratefully acknowledges the kind assistance of: *Richard E. Ahlborn,* Curator, Division of Ethnic and Western Cultural History, Smithsonian Institution; *Ricardo Alegría,* Director, Instituto de Cultura Puertorriqueña; *Nancy K. Beinke,* Architectural Historian, Historic American Buildings Survey; *Carleton I. Calkin,* Curator, Historic St. Augustine Preservation Board; *Irene Curbelo de Díaz,* President, Museo de Santos, San Juan; *Yvonne Lange,* Curator-in-Charge, Museum of International Folk Art of the Museum of New Mexico, Santa Fe; *Hélène Santiago; Robert L. Shalkop,* Assistant Director and Curator, Taylor Museum of the Colorado Springs Fine Arts Center; *Cecilia Steinfeldt,* Curator of History and Decorative Arts, Witte Memorial Museum, San Antonio; *Robert J. Stroessner,* Curator, New World Art, The Denver Art Museum; *Hilary Caws* and *Ken Oshima;* and especially the helpful cooperation of *E. Boyd,* Curator Emeritus, Spanish Colonial Art, Museum of New Mexico, Santa Fe.

Photographs are by Alfred Tamarin with the exception of those on pages 4-5, 6, 7, 13, 20, 21 (right), 24, 25, 29, 32, 33, 34, 35, 36-37, 38, 39.

Cover illustrations: (Front) *San Rafael,* New Mexican santo, 1835-1845, Collections in Museum of New Mexico. (Back) *Los Tres Santos Reyes,* Puerto Rican santo, twentieth century, Private Collection. Photographs by Alfred Tamarin.

1 2 3 4 5 6 7 8 9 10

El Niño Jesus, Puerto Rican santo, twentieth century, Museo de Santos, San Juan

Christopher Columbus found the New World in 1492 and claimed it for the King and Queen of Spain. Spanish explorers followed soon after, searching for treasure. In Mexico and Peru they found hoards of gold and silver. But there was no gold for the adventurers who turned northward to what is now the United States. The most famous of these explorers were Juan Ponce de León, Hernando de Soto and Francisco Vásquez de Coronado.

In time Spanish settlers spread through what are now the states of Florida, Texas, New Mexico, Colorado, Arizona and California. The island of Puerto Rico was settled even earlier. The colonists brought their European customs and crafts with them. They adapted to life in the new land and developed distinctive art forms, especially in New Mexico and Puerto Rico.

florida was discovered by Ponce de León in 1513. Ships filled with treasures from New Spain (Mexico) sailed along the coast of Florida on their voyage home to Spain. To protect the ships from pirates, the Spaniards built a *presidio,* or military fort, at St. Augustine, Florida. The fortress, called Castillo de San Marcos, was originally built of wood. Finally a strong fort was constructed of blocks of *coquina,* a stone formed of thousands of tiny sea shells fused together. Oyster shells were burned to make the mortar in which the blocks of coquina were set.

The Castillo has high walls surrounded by a moat, a deep ditch filled with water. Within the thick walls are living quarters, a chapel, dungeons, storerooms and guardrooms. Sixty-four guns were mounted on the walls.

The Castillo is the oldest stone fortress in the United States.

1696–1795,
Historic American Buildings Survey,
National Park Service

St. Augustine is the oldest permanent settlement by Europeans in what is now

the United States. The earliest governors lived in their own wooden houses.

When a central plaza, or square, was laid out in the town, the governor built a house

on the plaza, but it was burned down several times. Finally a two-story house of

coquina was constructed for use as the governor's residence and office, and as

a social center. A second-story balcony, the gabled, or peaked, roof and watch

tower can all be seen in the watercolor above.

The Spaniards in Mexico organized many expeditions that went northward to search for gold. In 1598 the explorer Juan de Oñate reported passing an Indian village in what is now Mesilla, New Mexico. Two hundred and fifty years later a Spanish village was established there. Below is a view of the town plaza in old Mesilla. The church and the simple one-story, flat-roofed houses are typical of adobe architecture in New Mexico. Spanish adobe houses are made of mud bricks. The mud is mixed with straw and the bricks are dried in the sun.

Mesilla became a resting place on the long journey from Texas to California. A donkey, covered wagon, stagecoach and *carreta,* or typical Spanish oxcart, are all moving along the street in the painting below.

Artist unknown, about 1880, oil, National Collection of Fine Arts, Smithsonian Institution, on loan to Museum of New Mexico

Before 1644

a lieutenant in Coronado's expedition, Hernando de Alvarado, visited the Indian village of Acoma, in New Mexico, in 1540. The village is built on top of a mesa, a flat plateau of rock, rising nearly four hundred feet above the surrounding plains. Acoma is called "City of the Sky." It was the scene of bitter battles between the Spaniards and the Pueblo Indians.

The church of San Estéban in Acoma was a mission, a station for the Roman Catholic priests who came to convert the Indians to Christianity. The church, which stands on a stone foundation, has walls of adobe and stone ten feet thick.

Two sturdy bell towers are on either side of the entrance. Attached to the church are living rooms, workrooms, storerooms, balconies and an inner patio. Wooden *vigas* can be seen in the walls. Vigas are large logs that stretch across a building and hold up the roof.

The San Estéban church was built by Franciscan friars. The Franciscans are a brotherhood of religious men who also built other churches in New Mexico, Texas and California. The Franciscan order was founded by St. Francis of Assisi, known to the Spaniards as San Francisco de Assís.

Francis was a wealthy young Italian who one day gave away all his fine clothes to a needy man. He had a vision and decided to give up his wealth. Francis spent the rest of his life helping others. He became known for his love for wild beasts and birds. He is shown here in a large painting on buffalo hide.

About 1700, Collections in Museum of New Mexico

The Spaniards who settled in New Mexico built one-story adobe houses. Below is a tiny wooden model of a New Mexican house. *Ristras,* long strings of chili peppers that are hung out to dry, make this model look like New Mexican houses of today. The tiny figures represent the story of the birth of Christ.

The early Spanish settlers in the New World were Roman Catholics who were used to highly decorated churches filled with paintings and statues. In America

About 1860, Collection of Mr. and Mrs. Charles W. Collier, Alcalde, New Mexico

they decorated their churches, family chapels and homes with *santos*. Santo is a Spanish word which means "holy image." Santos in the form of little statues are called *bultos*. Those painted on a flat surface are called *retablos*.

Santos are treated as members of the family. Women sew miniature clothing for them. They are included in festivals and feast days. People pray to them, hoping that the santos will help to have favors granted.

This little wooden bulto represents Barbara, who lived in Egypt in ancient times. Barbara's father was afraid that she would get married and leave him, so he kept her locked up in a tower. Barbara turned away from her religion and became a Christian. When her father heard this, he became so angry that he had her tortured and killed. Immediately a bolt of lightning struck him dead. Barbara is called upon for protection from lightning and storms.

About 1830, Taylor Museum of
Colorado Springs Fine Arts Center

Santiago el Major (Saint James the Greater) is the patron saint of Spain. Many centuries ago he is said to have helped drive out the Moors —Mohammedans from the Near East who occupied southern Spain for hundreds of years. "Santiago" was the battle cry of the Spanish *conquistadores,* or conquerors, in the New World. He is said to have come to the aid of the Spaniards fourteen different times when they were fighting Indians in America.

Santiago is shown at right riding a horse and carrying a sword. People often bring the figure miniature straw hats for his head and

1813–1816

tiny bridles for his horse. This bulto is in a glass case in a *santuario* (sanctuary), or small chapel, at Chimayó, New Mexico (at left).

This chapel has adobe walls covered with smooth plaster. The vigas that rest on the walls can be clearly seen. Smaller poles and mud are placed on top of the vigas to form the roof.

The Santuario at Chimayó is visited by thousands of sick and crippled people who believe that earth under the chapel is miraculous and can heal their illnesses. Many visiting pilgrims toss aside their canes and crutches after eating bits of this mud.

About 1817, photograph courtesy of Museum of New Mexico

The bultos at left represent a New Mexican version of the story of Joseph and Mary and the infant Jesus. Mary is dressed like a well-to-do Spanish woman in New Mexico about one hundred years ago. Her hands are pressed together in grief. In her breast can be seen a dagger, a symbol of the sorrows that she will have to suffer. Joseph holds the child on his arm. In his hand is a flowering staff.

The group of three figures at right represents the Trinity—God the Father, God the Son and God the Holy Spirit. Painted on their breasts are their symbols: a shining sun, a lamb and a dove.

New Mexican bultos usually measure about a foot and a half in height. The image maker, called a *santero,* carved them out of pine or the dried root of a cottonwood tree. The bodies were carved in one piece and the head and arms carved separately and attached by wood pegs.

The bultos were coated with a layer of gesso, a kind of plaster mixed with glue. Then they were painted with water colors and given a clear coat of varnish.

About 1800,
Collections in
Museum of New Mexico

ut 1870, Taylor Museum of
rado Springs Fine Arts Center

About 1850, Collection of Mr. and Mrs. Charles W. Collier, Alcalde, New Mexico

According to the story in the Bible, Adam and Eve were the first man and woman in the world. They lived in the Garden of Eden, where they had everything they needed. They were forbidden to taste the fruit of only one tree—the Tree of Knowledge of Good and Evil. However, the demon Satan in the form of a serpent tempted Eve to taste that fruit. At left, Eve is offering Adam an apple from the Tree of Knowledge.

Because they had eaten the forbidden fruit, Adam and Eve were driven out of the Garden of Eden, and the serpent, who had formerly walked on two legs, was condemned to crawl on its belly forever afterward.

Also in the Bible is the story of Abraham, who is called the father of the Jews. His wife Sarah was childless. Late in their lives they were visited by three angels who foretold that Sarah would become a mother. Sarah laughed because she thought that she was too old to have a child, but soon thereafter a son was born to her. He was named Isaac, or "Yitzhak," a Hebrew word meaning "to laugh."

This retablo shows the three angels who appeared to Abraham.

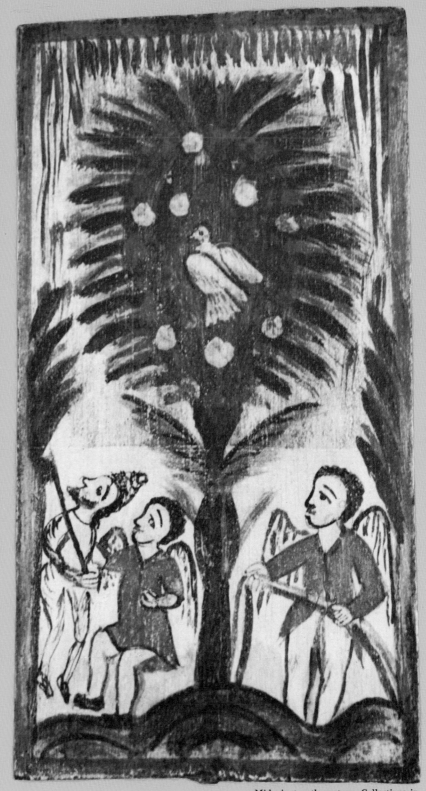

Mid nineteenth century, Collections in Museum of New Mexico

About 1835–1845, Taylor Museum of
Colorado Springs Fine Arts Center

San Miguel Arcángel (St. Michael the archangel, or one of the chief angels) was the patron saint of New Mexican soldiers. According to legend, the demon Satan was originally an angel in Heaven. When Satan revolted against God, Miguel led the fight against him. Satan was defeated and cast out from Heaven. This bulto of San Miguel shows him with wings. He has been given a real tin crown. His clothes are copied from European pictures. San Miguel is brandishing a sword over the fallen Satan. He is also holding scales, for it is his task to weigh the good and bad deeds of people.

Farmers of New Mexico look to San Ysidro Labrador (St. Isidore the farmer) to send rain and to guard their crops from pests. According to an old Spanish legend, Ysidro was a poor farmer who said such long prayers each morning that he was late for his work in the fields. While he was praying, an angel guided the farmer's oxen to plow the fields.

In the bulto at right, Ysidro is dressed in the working clothes of a New Mexican farmer of Spanish Colonial days. His coat and knee breeches are painted on him. Breeches were worn by New Mexican men until about 1830, when long pants came into use. Ysidro is wearing a miniature straw hat and tiny cloth boots decorated with beads.

About 1900, Collections in
Museum of New Mexico

In Spanish Colonial times, New Mexicans made almost everything by hand. Very few things could be imported. Supplies from Spain to the colonies had to go first to Mexico by ship. To reach New Mexico they had to be carried over difficult mountain trails in oxcarts.

The photograph above shows how the inside of a New Mexican adobe house looked in the eighteenth century. The floor was packed earth. There was very little furniture—only cupboards, carved chests on wooden stands, leather trunks and a few stools. People sat and slept on the floor. Clothes were hung on poles or kept in chests. Wooden grills covered the windows, which were small and set high in the wall. Thin sheets of mica took the place of glass. A large fireplace in the corner was used for cooking and heating.

The coarse rug, called a *jerga,* was woven in narrow strips and sewn together. Most of the pots and the *metate* and *mano* for grinding corn were made by Pueblo Indians.

Rawhide trunks were used for storage as well as for traveling. The one below is bound with iron bands and has metal locks. Ironwork was rare because metal was scarce. The shield is also made of leather. It is decorated with painted and stitched designs of a crown and the coat of arms of Spain.

Nineteenth century, Taylor Museum of
Colorado Springs Fine Arts Center

Late eighteenth century,
Smithsonian Institution

The first Spanish settlers in America brought sheep, which provided wool for cloth as well as mutton for food. To make woolen cloth, the sheep had to be sheared. Then the wool was carded, or combed, spun into thread on a handmade spinning wheel, washed with suds made from the roots of the yucca plant and woven into cloth.

New Mexican women embroidered designs on woolen cloth to be used as wall hangings for the village churches. The *colcha* stitch was used, so the hangings are called *colchas*. In later times colchas were used for curtains and bedspreads. The colcha at left is stitched with a double-headed eagle under a crown. The dyes for the woolen embroidery yarns were made from plants: indigo for blue, logwood (mahogany) for brown and the chamiso flower for yellow. Some colchas were embroidered on cotton.

There were no beds in early New Mexican homes. People slept on the floor wrapped up in blankets, sat on them and wore them outdoors. The blanket with the eight-pointed star below, left, is from El Valle, New Mexico, and is called a *vallero*. It was woven by a crippled girl whose father made her a special hand-operated loom. Spanish looms are usually operated by foot pedals. The blanket below, right, is from La Isla, Colorado.

About 1890, Collections in Museum of New Mexico

About 1910, Collections in Museum of New Mexico

About 1840–1860,
Collections in
Museum of New Mexico

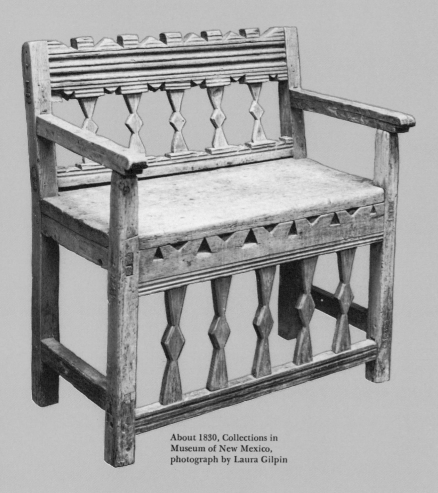

About 1830, Collections in
Museum of New Mexico,
photograph by Laura Gilpin

Church bells were very important to the early Spaniards in America. People did not have clocks or watches. The bells tolled the hour of the day. They also rang for important events like births and deaths. This one was made by a traveling bell caster, who went wherever people needed new bells. He got the metal by melting down old, cracked bells.

At left is a small bench carved of pine by a New Mexican craftsman.

In 1821 Mexico gained her independence from Spain. At that time New Mexico was still part of Mexico. The following year a trade route was opened from Independence, Missouri, to Santa Fe, New Mexico. Metal goods and manufactured articles moved freely overland from the north.

At right is an elegant New Mexican room of the nineteenth century. In it are a bed and small table and chairs, which were used mostly for guests. The *trastero*, or great cupboard, and the wooden chest on a stand are painted. Colchas are used as table cover, bedspread and curtains.

A round pottery dish imported from Mexico stands in the cupboard. Santos are everywhere. Two santos are in *nichos*, or small cabinets—one on the painted chest and one on the wall. Also on the wall is a tiny tin picture frame with candlesticks.

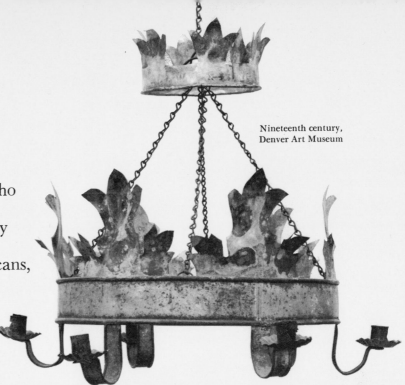

Nineteenth century,
Denver Art Museum

Large quantities of tin cans were brought into New Mexico with the soldiers of the United States Army, who used canned goods for food. The empty cans were salvaged by the New Mexicans, who cut them up and reshaped the metal into candleholders, picture frames and nichos for their santos.

The nicho at left contains El Santo Niño (the Holy Child) de Atocha, patron of prisoners. An old story tells that a group of prisoners were being held without food or water in a dungeon in Atocha, Spain. The Santo Niño appeared with a little basket of bread and a tiny gourd of water from which he provided an endless supply of food and drink for the prisoners.

It is said in New Mexico that the Santo Niño travels constantly through the countryside at night doing his good deeds. On his journeys he wears out many pairs of shoes, so people bring new shoes to the Niño.

Pieces of printed wallpaper decorate the frame of this nicho.

Above is a chandelier that held candles. Aside from the fireplace, candles were the only source of light in early New Mexican homes.

o about 1840, nicho 1880's,
ctions in Museum of New Mexico

Late eighteenth or early nineteenth century,
Taylor Museum of Colorado Springs
Fine Arts Center

Nuestra Señora de Guadalupe (Our Lady of Guadalupe) is a favorite saint of Spanish people. Often she is shown brown-skinned like the Mexican Indians. The shrine of Guadalupe in Mexico is built on a spot where the Virgin Mary is said to have appeared three times to a poor Indian named Juan Diego, telling him to have a church built there. At first no one would believe Juan. But a picture of Mary appeared on his cloak, which became filled with roses even though it was the middle of winter.

The retablo at left represents Our Lady of Guadalupe surrounded by the rays of the sun. She is standing on a crescent moon which is being held by an angel.

In New Mexico groups of men known as *Penitentes,* or "Brothers of Light," devote themselves to works of charity and care of the sick. On Good Friday they walk barefoot in a procession, dragging heavy crosses and whipping themselves, to imitate the traditional suffering of Jesus.

Carretas de las muertas (death carts), in which wooden skeletons sit, are kept in the Penitentes' *morada,* or meetinghouse. These figures have movable arms and legs. Dressed in black robes and long horsehair wigs, they are drawn in the Good Friday procession. During the procession, Penitentes chant and play the *pito,* a simple whistle.

About 1860, Taylor Museum of
Colorado Springs Fine Arts Center

About 1845,
Collections in
Museum of
New Mexico

a legend tells that Acacio (Achatius) was a Roman general in ancient times who became a Christian, then won a military victory. He made his soldiers become Christians also. Acacio was crucified by the Romans. Later he was made a saint, as is shown by the halo, or circle of light, around his head in this retablo. Although he was a Roman, Acacio wears the military uniform of an officer in New Spain. On either side of him are soldiers.

The retablo at right represents El Santo Niño Rey (Christ the King), dressed in nineteenth-century New Mexican clothes. He is seated on a throne and wearing a crown. His head is surrounded by a halo.

New Mexican retablos can be as small as six inches, or more than two feet high. They are cut from pine and covered with a layer of gesso. Like the bultos, they are given a coat of clear varnish after being painted with colors made mostly from plants.

Mid nineteenth century, Taylor Museum of
Colorado Springs Fine Arts Center

Texas was the third major area to be settled by the Spaniards in what is now

the United States. To prevent the French from occupying this land, the Spaniards

built military outposts and religious missions. One mission, founded at San Antonio,

was to become famous as the Alamo.

San Antonio de Valero (the Alamo) was no longer a mission when it became

the scene of a bloody battle between the American settlers of Texas and the soldiers of

the government of Mexico. In 1836, 188 Texans took refuge in the Alamo, which

was being used as a military fortress. The Alamo was demolished by the Mexican troops

under the leadership of General Antonio López de Santa Anna, and all the Americans

were killed. Among them was the famous Western scout, Davy Crockett. "Remember the Alamo" became the Texans' battle cry as they went on to win their independence from Mexico.

The old sketch at left shows all that remained of the mission after the battle. The richly carved entrance to the chapel can still be admired.

Life in a Spanish town centered around the plaza. The sketch below shows the main plaza in the city of San Antonio, the most important settlement in Spanish Texas. Nearby can be seen the San Fernando Cathedral and the stores and houses beside it.

Seth Eastman, 1849, pencil, The Peabody Museum, Harvard University

One of the most magnificent old churches in America is the mission church of San Xavier del Bac, on the outskirts of Tucson, Arizona. "Bac" is a Pima Indian word for "where the water flows beneath the ground."

San Xavier is in the style of Spanish and Mexican churches. Its domed roof, towers and molded portal, or entrance way, rise majestically over the flat Arizona desert. One of the bell towers was never finished. The church was constructed of burned bricks which were molded of clay, then hardened by fire. The walls are covered with white lime plaster.

1783–1797, photographs by Helga Teiwes, Arizona State Museum, University of Arizona

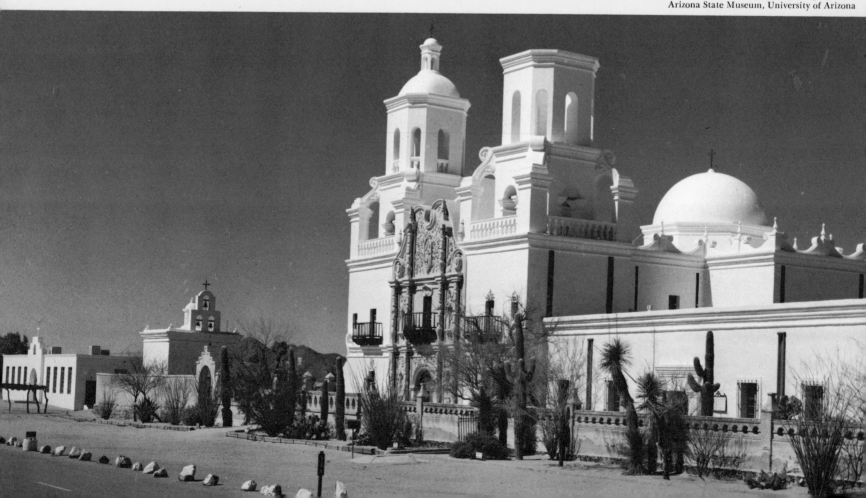

The entire interior of San Xavier is decorated. Above is a view of the main altar. The molded brick decorations were gilded, or covered with gold. The statue in the center is of San Xavier, patron saint of the mission. The body of the statue was made in Arizona, but the hands and head were imported from Mexico.

Spanish expeditions began exploring the Pacific Coast soon after the first Spaniards came to America. But California was not colonized until the middle of the eighteenth century. The Spaniards established missions in California to prevent the British and Russians from settling on the Pacific Coast.

Like other Spanish missions in America, the California missions were groups of buildings surrounded by a wall. Most important was the church. There also were buildings with cooking and storage rooms as well as living quarters. Outside the wall were fields of grain, fruit orchards and the water supply.

This drawing shows the San Luis Rey de Francia Mission, near Oceanside, shortly after it was built. It was constructed of adobe brick in the Spanish and Moorish style of architecture.

Built 1811–1815, lithograph 1840,
Library of Congress

Twenty-one California missions stretched about six hundred and fifty miles from the Mexican border to just north of San Francisco Bay. They were connected by *El Camino Real* (the Royal Road). The missions were spaced so that a traveler on horseback could go from one to the next in a single day.

Carmel was the headquarters for the two priests who founded most of the California missions, Junípero Serra and Fermín Francisco de Lasuén. The Mission of San Carlos de Borroméo in Carmel is shown below. The unusual star-shaped

Built 1793–1797, watercolor by William Smythe 1827,
The Peabody Museum, Harvard University

Santa Manuela Rancho, William Rich Hutton, 1851, pencil,
The Huntington Library, San Marino, California

window and the tall dome on one of the bell towers can be seen. The church was
built of blocks of sandstone set in mortar made of crushed abalone shells. The little
houses around the church are huts where the Indians lived.

The Spaniards brought horses to America, as well as the first cattle. Early
Spanish cowboys introduced Mexican-style ranching in California and made it an
important center for raising cattle. Many of the words used in modern-day ranching
are from the Spanish, such as lasso, rodeo, sombrero, chaparajos (chaps) and ranchero.

Above is a drawing of a one-story *hacienda,* or house, which set the style for
today's ranch houses. The long slanting roof extends over the huge veranda and helps
protect the adobe walls from rain.

Built 1719, restored 1965,
courtesy of Dr. and Mrs.
Ricardo E. Alegría

$\mathcal{T}$he island of Puerto Rico, which means "rich port," was a landing place for

Columbus on his second voyage to America in 1493. San Juan, Puerto Rico, has the

second-oldest Spanish church in America.

The narrow streets of San Juan are lined with lovely old houses that are

simple on the outside, with balconies on the second stories. Originally the ground

Courtesy of Dr. and Mrs.
Ricardo E. Alegría

floors were used for stables or rooms for servants. Today they are often occupied

by shops. Living quarters for the family are on the second floor. Like most houses in

Spanish America, this one has an inner patio, or courtyard.

Wood-burning cookstoves were used in the kitchen. The decorative tiles in this

San Juan kitchen are from Delft, Holland.

Second quarter of twentieth century, Smithsonian Institution

Small santos, usually less than a foot tall, are honored in Puerto Rican homes. The group above represents Ursula and her eleven thousand companions. According to legend, Ursula was a beautiful Christian princess. A pagan prince sought her hand in marriage, but Ursula made almost impossible demands before she would consent. She asked for ten noble maidens as companions, each of whom should be given a thousand handmaidens, and she must have a thousand of her own. She insisted that the wedding be delayed until she and her companions had made a pilgrimage to Rome. And she demanded that the prince and all of his court give up their pagan beliefs and become Christians.

The prince accepted Ursula's conditions and they all went to Rome together.

On their return journey the entire party was captured and killed except for Ursula. The enemy leader offered to spare her life if he could make her his queen, but she refused and was killed also.

Like most carved santos, Puerto Rican bultos have their hands and heads set into place separately. Over the years most of the hands have been lost.

At right is Queen Helena, the mother of the Roman Emperor Constantine. A story tells that Queen Helena made a journey to Jerusalem to find the wooden cross on which Christ was crucified. She found three crosses and made a test to decide which was the true cross. A very sick man was placed on each of the three crosses in turn. When he touched the true cross, he was immediately cured. Because of her hard work and faith, Helena was made a saint.

Paint is sometimes applied directly to Puerto Rican santos, without a coat of gesso. A santo may get a new coat of paint on its feast day or at Christmas. Or sometimes, when a prayer has been granted, a Puerto Rican repays his santo with a fresh coat of paint.

Second quarter of twentieth century,
Smithsonian Institution

This bulto illustrates a miraculous event which is said to have taken place in the Puerto Rican community of Hormigueros. According to local legend, a poor basket weaver went into the fields to cut reeds for his baskets, and was about to be attacked by a savage bull. The basket weaver called on Mary for help. She came to his rescue and forced the savage bull to its knees, saving the man's life. The santo is called *La Virgen de Hormigueros*.

The story of Tobias and San Rafael

Second quarter of twentieth century,
Collection of Carlos La Costa

Arcángel (St. Raphael the archangel) is a tale
of a son's devotion. Tobias's father was old and
slowly going blind. He sent his son to collect debts
due him. Tobias set out with his faithful dog,
but he lost his way. The archangel Raphael,
in the form of a man, came to Tobias's rescue
and guided him. Once the debts were collected,
the archangel told young Tobias to catch a fish
and smear its gall on his father's blind eyes.
The old man regained his sight and Raphael
revealed himself as an archangel.

Twentieth century,
Collection of Teodoro Vidal

The twelfth day after Christmas, on the sixth of January, Puerto Rico

celebrates the feast of *Los Tres Reyes* (the Three Kings). It is said that when

the Christ Child was born, a bright star appeared in the eastern heavens. The

star was seen by three wise men who are called Gaspar, Melchior and Balthazar.

Guided by the star, they brought presents to the newborn child.

On the eve of Three Kings' Day, santos of the wise men are carried

through the village streets in boxes decorated with flowers. Puerto Rican children gather grass and place it with water under their beds for the kings' hungry horses. In the morning they find gifts where the grass and water had been. The black king, who rides a white horse, is thought to be the most generous and to bring the best toys.

Three Kings' Day is a time to visit friends. In the evening there is singing, dancing, feasting and fireworks.

At right is a santo of Mary receiving the royal visitors and their gifts.

Santos are still being made today in Puerto Rico.

Second quarter of twentieth century,
Collection of Teodoro Vidal

Flight into Egypt, New Mexican woodcarving, early twentieth century, Collections in Museum of New Mexico

Puerto Rico was under Spanish control for four centuries. After the Spanish-American War in 1898, it became a commonwealth associated with the United States. All of the Spanish territories in the continental United States became states by 1912.

The heritage of Spain still lives today in Puerto Rico and the United States, centuries after the first conquistadores came to the New World. The Spanish language is the mother tongue of millions of Americans. The names of several states and many cities in the United States are Spanish.

New Mexicans continue to build adobe houses although nowadays they are likely to be filled with plastic statues of saints and factory-made furnishings. And a few churches, forts and public buildings from colonial times remain as symbols of the days when Spain dominated the New World.